50 Dairy-Free Japanese Dish Recipes for Home

By: Kelly Johnson

Table of Contents

- Sunomono (Cucumber salad)
- Tofu Salad with Sesame Dressing
- Kombu Dashi (Seaweed broth)
- Vegan Tamago (Japanese egg substitute)
- Vegan Kakiage (Mixed vegetable tempura)
- Vegan Miso Ramen
- Vegan Okonomiyaki (Japanese savory pancake)
- Tofu Poke Bowl
- Vegan Yudofu (Hot tofu in broth)
- Vegan Chawanmushi (Savory egg custard)
- Vegan Okonomiyaki (Japanese savory pancake)
- Vegan Karaage (Japanese fried mock meat)
- Vegan Nigiri Sushi
- Vegan Dorayaki (Sweet pancake with red bean paste)
- Vegan Matcha Tiramisu

Miso Soup

Ingredients:

- 4 cups water
- 3 tablespoons miso paste (white or red, depending on preference)
- 1 sheet dried seaweed (nori), cut into small pieces
- 1 block tofu, diced into small cubes
- 2 green onions (scallions), thinly sliced
- Optional: sliced mushrooms, tofu, spinach, or other vegetables of your choice

Instructions:

In a pot, bring the water to a simmer over medium heat.

Add the seaweed and tofu cubes to the pot and simmer for about 5 minutes, until the tofu is heated through and the seaweed is rehydrated.

In a small bowl, dilute the miso paste with a few tablespoons of hot water from the pot to create a smooth mixture.

Stir the diluted miso paste into the pot and reduce the heat to low. Be careful not to boil the soup once the miso is added, as it can affect the flavor.

Add any additional ingredients, such as sliced mushrooms or spinach, and simmer for another 2-3 minutes until they are cooked through.

Remove the pot from the heat and stir in the sliced green onions.

Taste the soup and adjust the seasoning if necessary, adding more miso paste for a stronger flavor or more water if it's too salty.

Serve the miso soup hot in bowls and enjoy!

Feel free to customize this recipe by adding your favorite ingredients, such as cooked noodles, sliced carrots, or even a splash of soy sauce for extra depth of flavor. Enjoy your homemade miso soup!

Sushi Rolls (with vegetables or seafood)

Ingredients:

- 2 cups sushi rice
- 2 1/2 cups water
- 1/3 cup rice vinegar
- 2 tablespoons sugar
- 1 teaspoon salt
- Nori seaweed sheets

Fillings:
For vegetable rolls: cucumber, avocado, carrot, bell pepper, or any other desired vegetables, thinly sliced

- For seafood rolls: cooked and seasoned sushi-grade fish (such as tuna or salmon), cooked shrimp, imitation crab, or any other desired seafood

Instructions:

Rinse the sushi rice under cold water until the water runs clear. Then, combine the rice and water in a rice cooker or pot and cook according to the package instructions.
In a small saucepan, heat the rice vinegar, sugar, and salt over low heat until the sugar and salt dissolve. Remove from heat and let it cool.
Once the rice is cooked, transfer it to a large bowl and gently fold in the vinegar mixture, being careful not to mash the rice. Allow the rice to cool to room temperature.
Place a sheet of nori shiny side down on a bamboo sushi rolling mat or a clean kitchen towel.
With wet hands, spread a thin layer of sushi rice evenly over the nori, leaving a small border along the top edge.
Arrange your desired fillings in a line across the center of the rice.
Starting from the bottom edge closest to you, tightly roll the sushi using the bamboo mat or towel, applying gentle pressure to shape it into a cylinder.
Once rolled, use a sharp knife to slice the sushi roll into bite-sized pieces.
Repeat the process with the remaining nori sheets and fillings.
Serve the sushi rolls with soy sauce, pickled ginger, and wasabi, if desired.

Enjoy your homemade sushi rolls, whether filled with colorful vegetables or delicious seafood!

Teriyaki Tofu

Ingredients:

- 1 block of firm tofu, drained and pressed to remove excess water
- 2 tablespoons soy sauce
- 2 tablespoons mirin (Japanese sweet rice wine)
- 1 tablespoon rice vinegar
- 1 tablespoon brown sugar
- 1 clove garlic, minced
- 1 teaspoon grated ginger
- 1 tablespoon vegetable oil
- Optional: sesame seeds and sliced green onions for garnish

Instructions:

Cut the tofu block into cubes or slices, depending on your preference.
In a small bowl, whisk together the soy sauce, mirin, rice vinegar, brown sugar, minced garlic, and grated ginger to make the teriyaki sauce.
Heat the vegetable oil in a large non-stick skillet over medium heat.
Add the tofu pieces to the skillet and cook for 3-4 minutes on each side, or until they are golden brown and slightly crispy.
Pour the teriyaki sauce over the tofu in the skillet, stirring gently to coat each piece evenly.
Allow the tofu to cook in the sauce for another 2-3 minutes, or until the sauce thickens and glazes the tofu.
Once the tofu is coated and heated through, remove the skillet from the heat.
Transfer the teriyaki tofu to a serving plate and garnish with sesame seeds and sliced green onions, if desired.
Serve the teriyaki tofu hot with steamed rice and your favorite vegetables.

Enjoy the flavorful and savory teriyaki tofu as a delicious main course or as a protein-packed addition to your favorite stir-fries and rice bowls!

Edamame Salad

Ingredients:

- 2 cups shelled edamame (fresh or frozen, thawed)
- 1 cup corn kernels (fresh or canned, drained)
- 1 red bell pepper, diced
- 1/2 cup diced cucumber
- 1/4 cup chopped red onion
- 1/4 cup chopped fresh cilantro or parsley
- 2 tablespoons rice vinegar
- 1 tablespoon soy sauce
- 1 tablespoon sesame oil
- 1 teaspoon honey or maple syrup (optional)
- Salt and pepper to taste
- Optional toppings: sliced green onions, sesame seeds

Instructions:

In a large mixing bowl, combine the shelled edamame, corn kernels, diced bell pepper, diced cucumber, chopped red onion, and chopped cilantro or parsley.
In a small bowl, whisk together the rice vinegar, soy sauce, sesame oil, and honey or maple syrup (if using) to make the dressing.
Pour the dressing over the edamame mixture in the large bowl and toss until everything is evenly coated.
Season the salad with salt and pepper to taste.
Cover the bowl and refrigerate the salad for at least 30 minutes to allow the flavors to meld together.
Before serving, give the salad a final toss and adjust the seasoning if necessary.
Garnish the edamame salad with sliced green onions and sesame seeds, if desired.
Serve chilled as a refreshing side dish or light lunch option.

Enjoy this vibrant and flavorful Edamame Salad packed with protein and vegetables, perfect for any occasion!

Vegetable Tempura

Ingredients:

- Assorted vegetables (such as bell peppers, zucchini, sweet potatoes, broccoli, and mushrooms), sliced into bite-sized pieces
- 1 cup all-purpose flour
- 1 cup ice-cold sparkling water or club soda
- 1/4 teaspoon baking powder
- Vegetable oil, for frying
- Salt, to taste
- Dipping sauce (such as soy sauce or tempura dipping sauce), for serving

Instructions:

Heat vegetable oil in a deep fryer or large pot to 350°F (180°C).
In a large mixing bowl, combine the all-purpose flour and baking powder.
Gradually add the ice-cold sparkling water or club soda to the flour mixture, whisking gently until just combined. Be careful not to overmix; some lumps are okay.
Dip the assorted vegetable pieces into the batter, coating them evenly.
Carefully place the battered vegetables into the hot oil, working in batches to avoid overcrowding the fryer or pot.
Fry the vegetables for 2-3 minutes, or until they are golden brown and crispy.
Use a slotted spoon or tongs to remove the vegetable tempura from the oil and transfer them to a plate lined with paper towels to drain excess oil.
Sprinkle the vegetable tempura with salt while they are still hot.
Serve the vegetable tempura immediately with your choice of dipping sauce on the side.

Enjoy the crispy and flavorful Vegetable Tempura as a delicious appetizer or side dish!

Gyoza (Japanese dumplings)

Ingredients:

- 1 pack gyoza wrappers (round or square)
- 250g ground pork (or substitute with ground chicken or tofu for a vegetarian option)
- 1 cup finely chopped cabbage
- 2 cloves garlic, minced
- 1 tablespoon fresh ginger, grated
- 2 tablespoons soy sauce
- 1 tablespoon sesame oil
- 1 tablespoon rice vinegar
- 1 teaspoon sugar
- 2 green onions, finely chopped
- Salt and pepper, to taste
- Water, for sealing dumplings
- Vegetable oil, for cooking

Instructions:

In a large mixing bowl, combine the ground pork, chopped cabbage, minced garlic, grated ginger, soy sauce, sesame oil, rice vinegar, sugar, chopped green onions, salt, and pepper. Mix well until all ingredients are thoroughly combined.
To assemble the gyoza, place a small spoonful of the filling in the center of a gyoza wrapper.
Moisten the edges of the wrapper with water using your finger.
Fold the wrapper in half over the filling, pressing the edges together to seal tightly. You can crimp the edges decoratively if desired.
Repeat the process until all the filling is used, making approximately 20-30 gyoza.
Heat a large non-stick skillet over medium heat and add a tablespoon of vegetable oil.
Arrange the gyoza in the skillet in a single layer, making sure they are not touching each other.
Cook the gyoza for 2-3 minutes, or until the bottoms are golden brown.
Carefully pour 1/4 cup of water into the skillet and immediately cover with a lid to steam the gyoza.
Steam the gyoza for 4-5 minutes, or until the filling is cooked through and the wrappers are translucent.

Remove the lid and continue cooking for another 1-2 minutes, or until the water has evaporated and the bottoms of the gyoza are crispy again.
Transfer the cooked gyoza to a serving plate and serve hot with your favorite dipping sauce, such as soy sauce mixed with rice vinegar, chili oil, or ponzu sauce.

Enjoy these homemade Gyoza as a delicious appetizer or main dish!

Chicken Yakitori

Ingredients:

- 500g boneless, skinless chicken thighs or breast, cut into bite-sized pieces
- 1/4 cup soy sauce
- 1/4 cup mirin (Japanese sweet rice wine)
- 2 tablespoons sake (Japanese rice wine) or dry white wine
- 2 tablespoons brown sugar
- 2 cloves garlic, minced
- 1 teaspoon grated ginger
- Bamboo skewers, soaked in water for 30 minutes

Instructions:

In a mixing bowl, combine the soy sauce, mirin, sake, brown sugar, minced garlic, and grated ginger to make the yakitori marinade.

Add the chicken pieces to the marinade, making sure they are evenly coated.

Cover the bowl and refrigerate for at least 30 minutes, or ideally for 1-2 hours, to allow the flavors to meld together.

Preheat your grill or broiler to medium-high heat.

Thread the marinated chicken pieces onto the soaked bamboo skewers, leaving a little space between each piece.

Grill or broil the chicken skewers for 5-6 minutes on each side, or until the chicken is cooked through and nicely charred on the outside.

While grilling, brush the chicken skewers with any remaining marinade to enhance the flavor and moisture.

Once the chicken is cooked, remove the skewers from the grill or broiler and transfer them to a serving plate.

Garnish the Chicken Yakitori with sliced green onions or sesame seeds, if desired.

Serve the Chicken Yakitori hot with steamed rice and a side of your favorite dipping sauce, such as teriyaki sauce or Japanese barbecue sauce.

Enjoy these flavorful and tender Chicken Yakitori skewers as a delicious appetizer or main dish at your next gathering or weeknight dinner!

Ramen Soup (using vegetable broth)

Ingredients:

- 4 cups vegetable broth
- 2 cups water
- 2 cloves garlic, minced
- 1 tablespoon ginger, grated
- 2 tablespoons soy sauce
- 1 tablespoon miso paste
- 1 tablespoon sesame oil
- 1 teaspoon rice vinegar
- 1 teaspoon sriracha or chili paste (adjust to taste)
- 200g ramen noodles
- Toppings (optional): sliced green onions, thinly sliced carrots, sliced mushrooms, spinach leaves, boiled eggs, nori seaweed, tofu cubes, corn kernels, bean sprouts, sesame seeds

Instructions:

In a large pot, combine the vegetable broth, water, minced garlic, grated ginger, soy sauce, miso paste, sesame oil, rice vinegar, and sriracha or chili paste. Bring to a simmer over medium heat, stirring occasionally.
Once the broth is simmering, reduce the heat to low and let it gently simmer for about 10-15 minutes to allow the flavors to meld together.
While the broth is simmering, cook the ramen noodles according to the package instructions. Drain and set aside.
Prepare your desired toppings by chopping and slicing them as needed.
To assemble the ramen bowls, divide the cooked noodles among serving bowls.
Ladle the hot broth over the noodles, making sure to distribute the garlic, ginger, and other flavorful ingredients evenly.
Arrange your desired toppings on top of the noodles and broth.
Garnish the ramen bowls with sliced green onions and sesame seeds, if desired.
Serve the Ramen Soup hot and enjoy immediately.

Feel free to customize your Ramen Soup with your favorite vegetables, protein, and toppings for a comforting and satisfying meal!

Onigiri (Japanese rice balls)

Ingredients:

- 2 cups sushi rice (short-grain Japanese rice)
- 2 1/2 cups water
- Salt, to taste
- Fillings (optional): salted salmon, pickled plum (umeboshi), cooked tuna, grilled chicken, seasoned vegetables, or any other desired fillings
- Nori seaweed sheets, cut into thin strips (optional)
- Sesame seeds (optional)

Instructions:

Rinse the sushi rice under cold water until the water runs clear. Then, drain the rice thoroughly.

In a rice cooker or pot, combine the rinsed rice and water. Cook the rice according to the package instructions.

Once the rice is cooked, let it cool slightly so it's easier to handle.

While the rice is still warm, season it with a pinch of salt, mixing gently to evenly distribute the salt.

Prepare your desired fillings by chopping or shredding them into small pieces.

To assemble the onigiri, wet your hands with water to prevent the rice from sticking. Take a small handful of rice and flatten it in the palm of your hand.

Place a small amount of your chosen filling in the center of the rice.

Fold the rice over the filling, shaping it into a triangle, ball, or cylindrical shape. Press firmly to compact the rice and seal the filling inside.

If using nori seaweed, wrap a strip of nori around the outside of the onigiri to secure it and add extra flavor.

Repeat the process with the remaining rice and fillings.

If desired, sprinkle sesame seeds over the onigiri for added flavor and texture.

Serve the onigiri immediately, or wrap them individually in plastic wrap for later enjoyment.

Onigiri makes a delicious and portable snack or light meal, perfect for picnics, lunchboxes, or on-the-go eating!

Nasu Dengaku (Miso-glazed eggplant)

Ingredients:

- 2 large Japanese eggplants or 1 large globe eggplant
- 2 tablespoons white miso paste
- 1 tablespoon mirin (Japanese sweet rice wine)
- 1 tablespoon sake (Japanese rice wine) or dry white wine
- 1 tablespoon sugar
- 1 tablespoon vegetable oil
- Optional garnish: sliced green onions, sesame seeds

Instructions:

Preheat your oven to 400°F (200°C). Line a baking sheet with parchment paper or aluminum foil.

Slice the eggplants in half lengthwise, then score the flesh in a criss-cross pattern with a sharp knife, being careful not to cut through the skin.

In a small bowl, whisk together the white miso paste, mirin, sake, and sugar to make the miso glaze.

Brush the cut side of each eggplant half with the miso glaze, ensuring that the flesh is evenly coated.

Place the glazed eggplant halves cut-side up on the prepared baking sheet.

Drizzle the vegetable oil over the eggplant halves to help them caramelize and become tender.

Roast the eggplant in the preheated oven for 20-25 minutes, or until the flesh is soft and the edges are caramelized and slightly charred.

Remove the eggplant from the oven and let it cool slightly.

Optional: Garnish the Nasu Dengaku with sliced green onions and sesame seeds for extra flavor and texture.

Serve the Nasu Dengaku warm as a flavorful side dish or appetizer.

Enjoy the rich and savory flavors of this Miso-glazed eggplant dish, perfect for a Japanese-inspired meal!

Okonomiyaki (Japanese savory pancake)

Ingredients:

- 2 cups shredded cabbage
- 1 cup all-purpose flour
- 2/3 cup dashi (Japanese soup stock) or water
- 2 eggs
- 4-6 strips of bacon or thinly sliced pork belly (optional)
- 1/2 cup thinly sliced green onions
- 1/4 cup tenkasu (tempura scraps, optional)
- 1/4 cup pickled red ginger (beni shoga, optional)
- Okonomiyaki sauce (or substitute with tonkatsu sauce)
- Japanese mayonnaise (or substitute with regular mayonnaise)
- Aonori (dried green seaweed flakes)
- Katsuobushi (bonito flakes)

Instructions:

In a large mixing bowl, combine the shredded cabbage, all-purpose flour, dashi or water, and eggs. Mix until well combined. The consistency should resemble a thick pancake batter.

Heat a non-stick skillet or griddle over medium heat. If using bacon or pork belly, cook it in the skillet until crispy. Remove and set aside.

Pour a ladleful of the okonomiyaki batter onto the skillet, spreading it into a circle about 1/2 inch thick.

If using, place a few slices of cooked bacon or pork belly on top of the batter.

Sprinkle some thinly sliced green onions, tenkasu, and pickled red ginger on top of the batter.

Cook the okonomiyaki for 4-5 minutes on each side, or until golden brown and cooked through.

Once cooked, transfer the okonomiyaki to a serving plate.

Drizzle okonomiyaki sauce and Japanese mayonnaise over the top in a crisscross pattern.

Sprinkle aonori and katsuobushi generously over the sauce.

Serve the okonomiyaki hot, either whole or sliced into wedges, with additional okonomiyaki sauce and mayonnaise on the side.

Enjoy this flavorful and customizable Japanese savory pancake as a delicious meal or snack!

Hiyayakko (Cold tofu salad)

Ingredients:

- 1 block (about 14 ounces) silken or soft tofu
- 2 green onions, thinly sliced
- 1 tablespoon grated ginger
- 2 tablespoons soy sauce
- 1 tablespoon sesame oil
- Optional toppings: bonito flakes (katsuobushi), shredded nori seaweed, sesame seeds, grated daikon radish, grated carrot, thinly sliced cucumber

Instructions:

Carefully remove the tofu from its packaging and drain any excess water. Pat the tofu dry with paper towels.

Slice the tofu into bite-sized cubes or rectangles and arrange them on a serving plate.

Sprinkle the thinly sliced green onions over the tofu.

In a small bowl, mix together the grated ginger, soy sauce, and sesame oil to make the dressing.

Drizzle the dressing over the tofu and green onions.

If desired, garnish the Hiyayakko with additional toppings such as bonito flakes, shredded nori seaweed, sesame seeds, grated daikon radish, grated carrot, or thinly sliced cucumber.

Serve the Hiyayakko immediately as a refreshing appetizer or light side dish.

Enjoy this simple and nutritious cold tofu salad, perfect for hot summer days or as a light and healthy addition to any Japanese meal!

Soba Noodle Salad

Ingredients:

For the salad:

- 200g soba noodles
- 1 cup shredded cabbage
- 1 carrot, julienned
- 1 red bell pepper, thinly sliced
- 1/2 cucumber, thinly sliced
- 2 green onions, thinly sliced
- 1/4 cup chopped fresh cilantro or parsley
- Optional: sliced radishes, shredded lettuce, snow peas, or any other desired vegetables

For the dressing:

- 3 tablespoons soy sauce
- 2 tablespoons rice vinegar
- 1 tablespoon sesame oil
- 1 tablespoon honey or maple syrup
- 1 teaspoon grated ginger
- 1 clove garlic, minced
- Optional: chili flakes or sriracha sauce for heat

Instructions:

Cook the soba noodles according to the package instructions. Drain and rinse the noodles under cold water to stop the cooking process and cool them down.
In a large mixing bowl, combine the cooked and cooled soba noodles with the shredded cabbage, julienned carrot, sliced bell pepper, sliced cucumber, sliced green onions, and chopped fresh cilantro or parsley. Add any additional vegetables you like.
In a small bowl, whisk together the soy sauce, rice vinegar, sesame oil, honey or maple syrup, grated ginger, minced garlic, and optional chili flakes or sriracha sauce to make the dressing.
Pour the dressing over the soba noodle salad and toss until everything is evenly coated.

Taste the salad and adjust the seasoning if necessary, adding more soy sauce, rice vinegar, or honey to taste.

Chill the soba noodle salad in the refrigerator for at least 30 minutes to allow the flavors to meld together.

Before serving, give the salad a final toss and garnish with additional chopped cilantro or parsley if desired.

Serve the soba noodle salad chilled as a refreshing and satisfying meal or side dish.

Enjoy this flavorful and nutritious Soba Noodle Salad, perfect for lunch, dinner, or as a potluck dish!

Tamagoyaki (Japanese rolled omelette)

Ingredients:

- 4 large eggs
- 2 tablespoons dashi (Japanese soup stock), or substitute with water
- 1 tablespoon soy sauce
- 1 tablespoon mirin (Japanese sweet rice wine)
- 1 teaspoon sugar
- Salt, to taste
- Vegetable oil for cooking

Instructions:

In a mixing bowl, beat the eggs until well combined.

Add the dashi (or water), soy sauce, mirin, sugar, and a pinch of salt to the beaten eggs. Mix until all ingredients are thoroughly incorporated.

Heat a Tamagoyaki pan or a small non-stick skillet over medium heat. Brush the inside of the pan with a little vegetable oil.

Pour a thin layer of the egg mixture into the pan, tilting the pan to spread the mixture evenly.

Once the bottom layer of the egg has set but is still slightly runny on top, start rolling it up from one end of the pan towards the other, using chopsticks or a spatula.

Push the rolled egg to the far end of the pan and brush the exposed part of the pan with oil.

Pour another thin layer of the egg mixture into the pan, lifting the rolled egg slightly to allow the new mixture to flow underneath.

Once the new layer has set slightly, roll it up along with the existing egg roll to create a thicker roll.

Repeat the process of rolling and adding layers until all of the egg mixture is used, forming a single rolled omelette.

Transfer the Tamagoyaki to a cutting board and let it cool slightly before slicing it into bite-sized pieces.

Serve the Tamagoyaki warm or at room temperature as a delicious side dish or part of a traditional Japanese breakfast.

Enjoy this classic and flavorful Tamagoyaki as a delightful addition to your meal!

Agedashi Tofu (Deep-fried tofu in broth)

Ingredients:

For the tofu:

- 1 block (about 14 ounces) firm tofu
- 1/4 cup cornstarch or potato starch
- Vegetable oil for frying

For the broth:

- 1 cup dashi (Japanese soup stock)
- 2 tablespoons soy sauce
- 1 tablespoon mirin (Japanese sweet rice wine)
- 1 tablespoon sake (Japanese rice wine) or dry white wine
- 1 teaspoon sugar
- Optional toppings: thinly sliced green onions, grated daikon radish, shredded nori seaweed, grated ginger

Instructions:

Start by preparing the tofu. Drain the tofu and wrap it in a clean kitchen towel or paper towels. Place a weight on top (such as a plate or a heavy pan) to press out excess moisture. Let it drain for about 20-30 minutes.

While the tofu is draining, prepare the broth. In a small saucepan, combine the dashi, soy sauce, mirin, sake, and sugar. Bring to a simmer over medium heat, then reduce the heat to low and let it simmer gently while you fry the tofu.

Cut the drained tofu into cubes or rectangles, about 1-inch thick.

Heat vegetable oil in a deep skillet or pot to 350°F (175°C).

Coat each tofu piece lightly in cornstarch or potato starch, shaking off any excess.

Carefully place the coated tofu pieces into the hot oil and fry until golden brown and crispy, about 3-4 minutes per side. Work in batches to avoid overcrowding the skillet.

Once the tofu is crispy and golden, remove it from the oil and drain on paper towels to remove excess oil.

To serve, place the fried tofu pieces in serving bowls or on a plate. Pour the hot broth over the tofu.

Garnish the Agedashi Tofu with thinly sliced green onions, grated daikon radish, shredded nori seaweed, and grated ginger, if desired.
Serve the Agedashi Tofu immediately as an appetizer or part of a Japanese meal.

Enjoy the crispy exterior and soft interior of this classic Agedashi Tofu dish, served in a flavorful and aromatic broth!

Daikon Radish Salad

Ingredients:

- 1 large daikon radish
- 2 tablespoons rice vinegar
- 1 tablespoon soy sauce
- 1 teaspoon sugar
- 1 teaspoon sesame oil
- Optional toppings: sesame seeds, thinly sliced green onions, shredded carrots, sliced cucumber

Instructions:

Peel the daikon radish and cut it into thin matchstick-like strips or shred it using a grater.

Place the shredded daikon radish in a large bowl.

In a small bowl, whisk together the rice vinegar, soy sauce, sugar, and sesame oil to make the dressing.

Pour the dressing over the shredded daikon radish and toss until well coated.

Let the daikon radish salad marinate in the dressing for at least 15-20 minutes to allow the flavors to meld together.

Before serving, garnish the salad with optional toppings such as sesame seeds, thinly sliced green onions, shredded carrots, or sliced cucumber.

Serve the Daikon Radish Salad chilled as a refreshing side dish or appetizer.

Enjoy the crisp and tangy flavors of this Daikon Radish Salad, perfect for accompanying a variety of Asian-inspired meals!

Chirashi Sushi (Scattered sushi)

Ingredients:

For the sushi rice:

- 2 cups sushi rice
- 2 cups water
- 1/4 cup rice vinegar
- 2 tablespoons sugar
- 1 teaspoon salt

For the toppings (can be customized to your preference):

- Sashimi-grade fish (such as tuna, salmon, yellowtail)
- Cooked shrimp, crab meat, or scallops
- Assorted vegetables (such as cucumber, avocado, radish sprouts, shredded carrots)
- Tamagoyaki (Japanese rolled omelette), sliced into thin strips
- Nori seaweed, cut into thin strips
- Sesame seeds, for garnish
- Pickled ginger (gari) and wasabi, for serving

Instructions:

Rinse the sushi rice under cold water until the water runs clear. Drain the rice thoroughly.

In a rice cooker or pot, combine the sushi rice and water. Cook the rice according to the package instructions.

In a small saucepan, combine the rice vinegar, sugar, and salt. Heat over low heat, stirring until the sugar and salt are dissolved. Remove from heat and let it cool.

Once the rice is cooked, transfer it to a large mixing bowl. Gently fold in the seasoned rice vinegar, being careful not to mash the rice. Let the rice cool to room temperature.

While the rice is cooling, prepare your toppings by slicing the fish, cooking the shrimp or crab meat, and cutting the vegetables into thin strips.

To assemble the Chirashi Sushi, spread the sushi rice in a large serving bowl or individual bowls.
Arrange the sliced fish, cooked seafood, vegetables, and tamagoyaki on top of the rice in an attractive pattern.
Garnish the Chirashi Sushi with nori seaweed strips and sesame seeds.
Serve the Chirashi Sushi with pickled ginger and wasabi on the side.
Enjoy your homemade Chirashi Sushi as a colorful and flavorful meal!

Feel free to customize the toppings according to your preferences and availability.

Chirashi Sushi is versatile and can be adapted to include your favorite ingredients for a delicious and satisfying meal.

Sunomono (Japanese cucumber salad)

Ingredients:

- 2 Japanese cucumbers or 1 English cucumber, thinly sliced
- 1/4 cup rice vinegar
- 2 tablespoons sugar
- 1/2 teaspoon salt
- 1 teaspoon soy sauce
- 1 teaspoon sesame oil
- Optional garnish: sesame seeds, thinly sliced green onions, shredded nori seaweed

Instructions:

Place the thinly sliced cucumbers in a mixing bowl.

In a separate small bowl, whisk together the rice vinegar, sugar, salt, soy sauce, and sesame oil until the sugar and salt are dissolved.

Pour the dressing over the sliced cucumbers and toss until the cucumbers are evenly coated.

Let the cucumber salad marinate in the dressing for at least 15-20 minutes in the refrigerator to allow the flavors to meld together.

Before serving, garnish the Sunomono with optional toppings such as sesame seeds, thinly sliced green onions, or shredded nori seaweed.

Serve the Sunomono chilled as a refreshing side dish or appetizer.

Enjoy the crisp and tangy flavors of this Japanese cucumber salad, perfect for

accompanying a variety of Asian-inspired meals or as a light and refreshing snack!

Nikujaga (Japanese meat and potato stew)

Ingredients:

- 1 lb thinly sliced beef (such as beef for shabu-shabu or sukiyaki)
- 2 large potatoes, peeled and cut into chunks
- 1 large onion, thinly sliced
- 2 carrots, peeled and sliced into thick rounds
- 1 cup sliced mushrooms (optional)
- 4 cups dashi (Japanese soup stock), or substitute with beef or vegetable broth
- 1/4 cup soy sauce
- 2 tablespoons mirin (Japanese sweet rice wine)
- 2 tablespoons sugar
- 2 tablespoons vegetable oil
- Salt and pepper to taste
- Thinly sliced green onions for garnish

Instructions:

In a large pot or Dutch oven, heat the vegetable oil over medium heat. Add the thinly sliced beef and cook until browned on all sides.
Add the sliced onions to the pot and cook until they are softened and translucent.
Add the potatoes, carrots, and mushrooms (if using) to the pot.
Pour the dashi (or broth) over the ingredients in the pot.
Add the soy sauce, mirin, and sugar to the pot. Stir to combine.
Bring the mixture to a boil, then reduce the heat to low and cover the pot with a lid.
Simmer the Nikujaga for about 20-25 minutes, or until the potatoes and carrots are tender and cooked through.
Taste the stew and adjust the seasoning with salt and pepper if necessary.
Once the stew is cooked and the vegetables are tender, remove the pot from the heat.
Serve the Nikujaga hot, garnished with thinly sliced green onions.

Enjoy the rich and savory flavors of this comforting Nikujaga stew, perfect for a cozy meal on a chilly day!

Hijiki Salad (Seaweed salad)

Ingredients:

- 1/2 cup dried hijiki seaweed
- 1 carrot, julienned
- 1/2 cup sliced shiitake mushrooms
- 1/4 cup soy sauce
- 2 tablespoons mirin (Japanese sweet rice wine)
- 1 tablespoon sugar
- 1 tablespoon sesame oil
- 1 tablespoon rice vinegar
- 1 teaspoon grated ginger
- 1 clove garlic, minced
- 1 tablespoon sesame seeds, toasted
- Thinly sliced green onions, for garnish (optional)

Instructions:

Rinse the dried hijiki seaweed under cold water to remove any sand or debris. Place the rinsed hijiki in a bowl and cover with warm water. Let it soak for about 15-20 minutes, or until rehydrated. Drain well and set aside.

In a small bowl, combine the soy sauce, mirin, sugar, sesame oil, rice vinegar, grated ginger, and minced garlic to make the dressing. Whisk until the sugar is dissolved.

Heat a small amount of oil in a skillet over medium heat. Add the julienned carrot and sliced shiitake mushrooms, and sauté until softened.

Add the rehydrated hijiki seaweed to the skillet with the vegetables and continue to cook for another 2-3 minutes.

Pour the dressing over the hijiki mixture in the skillet and toss until everything is evenly coated. Cook for another minute to allow the flavors to meld together.

Remove the skillet from the heat and transfer the hijiki salad to a serving bowl. Sprinkle the toasted sesame seeds over the top of the salad.

Garnish the Hijiki Salad with thinly sliced green onions, if desired.

Serve the salad warm or at room temperature as a delicious side dish or appetizer.

Enjoy the unique and savory flavors of this Hijiki Salad, packed with nutritious seaweed and vegetables!

Yaki Udon (Stir-fried udon noodles)

Ingredients:

- 8 oz fresh or cooked udon noodles
- 1/2 lb thinly sliced protein (such as chicken, beef, shrimp, or tofu)
- 1 onion, thinly sliced
- 1 bell pepper, thinly sliced
- 1 carrot, julienned
- 2 cups shredded cabbage
- 2-3 tablespoons vegetable oil
- 2 cloves garlic, minced
- 1 tablespoon grated ginger
- 3 tablespoons soy sauce
- 1 tablespoon oyster sauce (optional)
- 1 tablespoon mirin (Japanese sweet rice wine)
- 1 teaspoon sesame oil
- Salt and pepper to taste
- Thinly sliced green onions and sesame seeds for garnish

Instructions:

If using fresh udon noodles, cook them according to the package instructions. If using cooked udon noodles, rinse them under cold water to separate the strands.
In a large skillet or wok, heat 1 tablespoon of vegetable oil over medium-high heat. Add the thinly sliced protein (chicken, beef, shrimp, or tofu) and stir-fry until cooked through. Remove the cooked protein from the skillet and set aside.
In the same skillet, add another tablespoon of vegetable oil if needed. Add the minced garlic and grated ginger, and stir-fry for about 30 seconds until fragrant.
Add the sliced onion, bell pepper, carrot, and shredded cabbage to the skillet. Stir-fry for 3-4 minutes until the vegetables are tender-crisp.
Return the cooked protein to the skillet with the vegetables.
Add the cooked udon noodles to the skillet, along with the soy sauce, oyster sauce (if using), mirin, and sesame oil. Stir-fry everything together until well combined and heated through.
Taste the Yaki Udon and adjust the seasoning with salt and pepper if needed.
Once everything is heated through and well mixed, remove the skillet from the heat.

Serve the Yaki Udon hot, garnished with thinly sliced green onions and sesame seeds.

Enjoy this flavorful and satisfying Yaki Udon as a delicious and comforting meal! Feel free to customize the ingredients and adjust the seasonings to suit your taste preferences.

Kabocha Squash Soup

Ingredients:

- 1 medium kabocha squash (about 2-3 pounds)
- 1 onion, chopped
- 2 cloves garlic, minced
- 4 cups vegetable broth
- 1 cup coconut milk (or substitute with heavy cream or almond milk for a lighter version)
- 2 tablespoons olive oil
- 1 teaspoon ground ginger
- 1/2 teaspoon ground cinnamon
- Salt and pepper to taste
- Optional garnish: toasted pumpkin seeds, drizzle of coconut milk, chopped fresh herbs (such as parsley or cilantro)

Instructions:

Preheat your oven to 400°F (200°C).

Cut the kabocha squash in half and remove the seeds and stringy fibers using a spoon. Cut the squash into smaller chunks and place them on a baking sheet lined with parchment paper.

Drizzle the squash with olive oil and sprinkle with salt and pepper. Roast in the preheated oven for about 40-45 minutes, or until the squash is tender and caramelized around the edges.

While the squash is roasting, heat 2 tablespoons of olive oil in a large pot over medium heat. Add the chopped onion and minced garlic, and sauté until softened and fragrant, about 5-7 minutes.

Once the squash is roasted, remove it from the oven and let it cool slightly. Use a spoon to scoop the flesh from the skin and add it to the pot with the sautéed onions and garlic.

Add the vegetable broth, ground ginger, and ground cinnamon to the pot. Stir to combine.

Bring the soup to a simmer, then reduce the heat to low and let it simmer gently for about 15-20 minutes to allow the flavors to meld together.

Use an immersion blender or transfer the soup in batches to a blender to puree until smooth.

Once the soup is smooth, stir in the coconut milk (or your preferred alternative) until well combined. Taste and adjust the seasoning with salt and pepper if needed.

Serve the Kabocha Squash Soup hot, garnished with toasted pumpkin seeds, a drizzle of coconut milk, and chopped fresh herbs if desired.

Enjoy this creamy and flavorful Kabocha Squash Soup as a comforting and nutritious meal!

Kinpira Gobo (Braised burdock root and carrot)

Ingredients:

- 2 burdock roots (gobo)
- 1 large carrot
- 2 tablespoons vegetable oil
- 2 tablespoons soy sauce
- 1 tablespoon mirin (Japanese sweet rice wine)
- 1 tablespoon sugar
- 1 teaspoon sesame oil
- Toasted sesame seeds for garnish (optional)
- Thinly sliced green onions for garnish (optional)

Instructions:

Peel the burdock roots (gobo) and carrot. Cut them into thin matchstick-like strips or julienne them.

Heat the vegetable oil in a large skillet or wok over medium heat.

Add the julienned burdock root to the skillet and stir-fry for about 2-3 minutes.

Add the julienned carrot to the skillet and continue to stir-fry for another 2-3 minutes.

In a small bowl, mix together the soy sauce, mirin, and sugar to make the sauce.

Pour the sauce over the burdock root and carrot in the skillet. Stir to combine.

Continue to cook, stirring occasionally, until the vegetables are tender and the sauce has thickened slightly, about 5-7 minutes.

Once the vegetables are cooked through, drizzle the sesame oil over the Kinpira Gobo and stir to coat evenly.

Transfer the Kinpira Gobo to a serving dish and garnish with toasted sesame seeds and thinly sliced green onions, if desired.

Serve the Kinpira Gobo hot or at room temperature as a delicious side dish or appetizer.

Enjoy the unique and savory flavors of this Kinpira Gobo, a classic Japanese dish that pairs well with rice and other Asian-inspired dishes!

Vegan Sashimi (using vegetables or tofu)

Ingredients:

For the marinade:

- 1/4 cup soy sauce
- 2 tablespoons rice vinegar
- 1 tablespoon mirin (Japanese sweet rice wine)
- 1 tablespoon sesame oil
- 1 teaspoon grated ginger
- 1 teaspoon sugar
- Optional: wasabi paste and pickled ginger for serving

For the vegan sashimi:

- 1 block extra-firm tofu, pressed and drained
- 1 large carrot
- 1 small daikon radish
- 1/2 English cucumber
- 1 sheet nori seaweed
- Optional garnish: thinly sliced green onions, sesame seeds

Instructions:

In a small bowl, whisk together the soy sauce, rice vinegar, mirin, sesame oil, grated ginger, and sugar to make the marinade. Set aside.

Slice the tofu into thin rectangular pieces, resembling the shape and size of sashimi slices. Place the tofu slices in a shallow dish and pour the marinade over them. Let the tofu marinate for at least 30 minutes, flipping halfway through to ensure even marination.

While the tofu is marinating, prepare the vegetables. Use a vegetable peeler or mandoline slicer to thinly slice the carrot, daikon radish, and cucumber into long, thin strips, resembling sashimi slices.

Cut the nori seaweed sheet into thin strips to use as garnish for the vegan sashimi.

Once the tofu has finished marinating, arrange the marinated tofu slices on a serving platter.

Top each tofu slice with a few slices of the prepared carrot, daikon radish, and cucumber to resemble traditional sashimi.

Garnish the vegan sashimi with nori seaweed strips, thinly sliced green onions, and sesame seeds, if desired.

Serve the vegan sashimi with a side of wasabi paste and pickled ginger for dipping, if desired.

Enjoy this creative and delicious Vegan Sashimi as a light and refreshing appetizer or part of a Japanese-inspired meal!

Tofu Dengaku (Miso-glazed tofu)

Ingredients:

- 1 block firm or extra-firm tofu
- 2 tablespoons white miso paste
- 1 tablespoon mirin (Japanese sweet rice wine)
- 1 tablespoon sake (Japanese rice wine) or dry white wine
- 1 tablespoon sugar
- 1 tablespoon sesame oil
- Optional garnish: toasted sesame seeds, thinly sliced green onions

Instructions:

Preheat your oven to 400°F (200°C). Line a baking sheet with parchment paper or aluminum foil.

Drain the tofu and cut it into thick slices or cubes.

In a small bowl, whisk together the white miso paste, mirin, sake, sugar, and sesame oil to make the miso glaze.

Place the tofu slices or cubes on the prepared baking sheet.

Brush the miso glaze over the tofu slices or cubes, coating them evenly.

Bake the tofu in the preheated oven for about 20-25 minutes, or until the tofu is golden brown and the miso glaze is caramelized.

Once the tofu is cooked and glazed, remove it from the oven and let it cool slightly.

Transfer the tofu to a serving plate and garnish with toasted sesame seeds and thinly sliced green onions, if desired.

Serve the Tofu Dengaku warm as a delicious appetizer or part of a Japanese-inspired meal.

Enjoy the rich and savory flavors of this Tofu Dengaku, perfect for tofu lovers and those seeking a tasty vegetarian or vegan dish!

Katsu Curry (Japanese curry with breaded cutlet)

Ingredients:

For the curry sauce:

- 2 tablespoons vegetable oil
- 1 onion, finely chopped
- 2 cloves garlic, minced
- 2 carrots, diced
- 2 potatoes, diced
- 3 cups vegetable or chicken broth
- 3 tablespoons curry powder
- 2 tablespoons soy sauce
- 1 tablespoon tomato paste
- 1 tablespoon honey or sugar
- Salt and pepper to taste

For the breaded cutlets (tonkatsu):

- 4 boneless pork loin chops or chicken breasts
- Salt and pepper to taste
- 1/2 cup all-purpose flour
- 2 large eggs, beaten
- 1 cup panko breadcrumbs
- Vegetable oil for frying

For serving:

- Cooked Japanese rice
- Thinly sliced cabbage or shredded lettuce
- Pickled ginger (optional)
- Japanese-style mayonnaise (optional)

Instructions:

Prepare the curry sauce: Heat the vegetable oil in a large pot over medium heat. Add the chopped onion and minced garlic, and sauté until softened and fragrant. Add the diced carrots and potatoes to the pot and cook for a few minutes. Pour in the vegetable or chicken broth and bring to a simmer. Cook until the vegetables are tender, about 15-20 minutes.

Stir in the curry powder, soy sauce, tomato paste, honey or sugar, salt, and pepper. Simmer for another 5-10 minutes to allow the flavors to meld together. Adjust seasoning if needed. Remove from heat and set aside.

Prepare the breaded cutlets (tonkatsu): Season the pork loin chops or chicken breasts with salt and pepper.

Set up a breading station with three shallow bowls: one containing the all-purpose flour, one containing the beaten eggs, and one containing the panko breadcrumbs.

Dredge each pork or chicken piece in the flour, shaking off any excess. Dip them into the beaten eggs, then coat them evenly with the panko breadcrumbs, pressing gently to adhere.

Heat vegetable oil in a large skillet over medium-high heat. Fry the breaded cutlets until golden brown and cooked through, about 4-5 minutes per side for pork and 3-4 minutes per side for chicken. Drain on paper towels.

Slice the cooked cutlets into strips.

To serve, spoon the curry sauce over a bed of cooked Japanese rice. Arrange the sliced cabbage or shredded lettuce on the side. Place the sliced breaded cutlets on top of the curry sauce.

Garnish with pickled ginger and a dollop of Japanese-style mayonnaise if desired.

Serve the Katsu Curry hot and enjoy the delicious flavors!

Enjoy this hearty and comforting Katsu Curry, a beloved Japanese dish that's sure to satisfy your cravings!

Yakisoba (Stir-fried noodles with vegetables)

Ingredients:

- 8 oz Yakisoba noodles (or substitute with ramen noodles or spaghetti)
- 1 tablespoon vegetable oil
- 1 onion, thinly sliced
- 2 cloves garlic, minced
- 1 carrot, julienned
- 1 bell pepper, thinly sliced
- 2 cups shredded cabbage
- 1 cup bean sprouts
- 2 green onions, chopped
- 1/4 cup Yakisoba sauce (see recipe below)
- Salt and pepper to taste
- Optional garnish: toasted sesame seeds, shredded nori seaweed, pickled ginger

For the Yakisoba sauce:

- 3 tablespoons soy sauce
- 2 tablespoons Worcestershire sauce
- 1 tablespoon ketchup
- 1 tablespoon oyster sauce (optional)
- 1 tablespoon mirin (Japanese sweet rice wine)
- 1 teaspoon sugar

Instructions:

Cook the Yakisoba noodles according to the package instructions. Drain and rinse the noodles under cold water to stop the cooking process. Set aside.
In a small bowl, whisk together all the ingredients for the Yakisoba sauce until well combined. Set aside.
Heat the vegetable oil in a large skillet or wok over medium-high heat.
Add the thinly sliced onion and minced garlic to the skillet. Stir-fry for about 1-2 minutes until fragrant.
Add the julienned carrot, thinly sliced bell pepper, shredded cabbage, and bean sprouts to the skillet. Stir-fry for another 3-4 minutes until the vegetables are tender-crisp.

Add the cooked Yakisoba noodles to the skillet. Pour the Yakisoba sauce over the noodles and vegetables. Toss everything together until well combined and heated through.
Season with salt and pepper to taste.
Once everything is heated through and well mixed, remove the skillet from the heat.
Serve the Yakisoba hot, garnished with chopped green onions and optional toppings such as toasted sesame seeds, shredded nori seaweed, or pickled ginger.

Enjoy this savory and satisfying Yakisoba, a flavorful Japanese noodle dish that's perfect for a quick and delicious meal!

Horenso Goma-ae (Spinach with sesame dressing)

Ingredients:

- 1 bunch of spinach
- 2 tablespoons soy sauce
- 1 tablespoon sugar
- 1 tablespoon mirin (Japanese sweet rice wine)
- 2 tablespoons sesame seeds
- 1 teaspoon sesame oil

Instructions:

Wash the spinach thoroughly and remove any tough stems. Bring a pot of water to a boil.

Blanch the spinach in the boiling water for about 1-2 minutes until wilted and bright green.

Drain the spinach and immediately transfer it to a bowl of ice water to stop the cooking process. Once cooled, squeeze out excess water from the spinach and set aside.

In a dry skillet, toast the sesame seeds over medium heat until fragrant and lightly browned, about 2-3 minutes. Remove from heat and let them cool slightly.

Grind the toasted sesame seeds in a mortar and pestle or spice grinder until finely ground. Alternatively, you can use a food processor.

In a small bowl, mix together the ground sesame seeds, soy sauce, sugar, mirin, and sesame oil to make the dressing.

Place the blanched spinach in a serving dish and drizzle the sesame dressing over the top.

Toss the spinach gently to coat it evenly with the dressing.

Serve the Horenso Goma-ae as a delicious side dish or part of a traditional Japanese meal.

Enjoy the nutty flavor and delicate texture of this Horenso Goma-ae, a classic Japanese dish that's both nutritious and satisfying!

Zaru Soba (Cold buckwheat noodles)

Ingredients:

For the soba noodles:

- 8 oz soba noodles (Japanese buckwheat noodles)
- Water for boiling
- Ice water for cooling

For the dipping sauce (Tsuyu):

- 1/2 cup soy sauce
- 1/2 cup mirin (Japanese sweet rice wine)
- 2 cups dashi (Japanese soup stock)
- 1 tablespoon sugar (optional)
- Thinly sliced green onions and grated daikon radish for garnish (optional)

Instructions:

Cook the soba noodles according to the package instructions in a pot of boiling water. It usually takes about 5-7 minutes for soba noodles to cook until they are tender but still firm to the bite.

Once the soba noodles are cooked, drain them and immediately rinse them under cold running water or plunge them into a bowl of ice water to stop the cooking process and cool them down quickly. Drain well.

Arrange the cooled soba noodles on a bamboo or wire rack set over a baking sheet or on individual plates.

Prepare the dipping sauce (Tsuyu): In a small saucepan, combine the soy sauce, mirin, dashi, and sugar (if using). Bring the mixture to a simmer over medium heat, then remove from heat and let it cool to room temperature.

Pour the dipping sauce into individual serving bowls.

Garnish the dipping sauce with thinly sliced green onions and grated daikon radish, if desired.

Serve the Zaru Soba noodles alongside the dipping sauce.

To eat, take a small portion of soba noodles and dip them into the dipping sauce before enjoying.

Enjoy the cool and refreshing flavors of Zaru Soba, perfect for hot summer days or as a light and healthy meal option!

Vegan Tonkatsu (Breaded and fried mock meat)

Ingredients:

For the mock meat:

- 4 pieces of vegan meat substitute (such as seitan cutlets, tofu cutlets, or tempeh)
- Salt and pepper to taste
- All-purpose flour for dredging
- Vegan egg substitute (such as flaxseed meal or chickpea flour mixed with water)
- Panko breadcrumbs for coating
- Vegetable oil for frying

For the Tonkatsu sauce:

- 1/4 cup ketchup
- 2 tablespoons soy sauce
- 1 tablespoon Worcestershire sauce (make sure it's vegan)
- 1 tablespoon mirin (Japanese sweet rice wine)
- 1 teaspoon sugar
- 1/2 teaspoon grated ginger (optional)

Instructions:

If using tofu or tempeh, press them to remove excess moisture. Season the mock meat with salt and pepper.

Set up a breading station with three shallow bowls: one containing all-purpose flour, one containing the vegan egg substitute, and one containing panko breadcrumbs.

Dredge each piece of mock meat in the flour, shaking off any excess. Dip them into the vegan egg substitute, then coat them evenly with the panko breadcrumbs, pressing gently to adhere.

Heat vegetable oil in a large skillet over medium-high heat.

Once the oil is hot, carefully add the breaded mock meat to the skillet. Fry until golden brown and crispy, about 3-4 minutes per side.

Remove the fried mock meat from the skillet and drain on paper towels to remove excess oil.

In a small saucepan, combine all the ingredients for the Tonkatsu sauce. Bring to a simmer over medium heat, then reduce the heat to low and let it simmer gently for a few minutes to thicken slightly.

Serve the vegan Tonkatsu hot, sliced into pieces, with the Tonkatsu sauce drizzled over the top.

Optionally, serve with shredded cabbage and rice on the side.

Enjoy the crispy and flavorful Vegan Tonkatsu, served with a savory and tangy Tonkatsu sauce, for a satisfying Japanese-inspired meal!

Nasu Agebitashi (Deep-fried eggplant in dashi broth)

Ingredients:

For the eggplant:

- 2 Japanese eggplants (or 1 large regular eggplant)
- Salt for sprinkling
- All-purpose flour for dredging
- Vegetable oil for frying

For the dashi broth:

- 2 cups dashi (Japanese soup stock)
- 2 tablespoons soy sauce
- 1 tablespoon mirin (Japanese sweet rice wine)
- 1 tablespoon sake (Japanese rice wine)
- 1 teaspoon sugar

For garnish:

- Thinly sliced green onions
- Toasted sesame seeds
- Shichimi togarashi (Japanese seven spice blend)

Instructions:

Prepare the eggplant: Cut the eggplant(s) into thick slices, about 1/2 inch thick. Sprinkle the slices with salt and let them sit for about 15-20 minutes to draw out excess moisture. After 20 minutes, pat the eggplant slices dry with paper towels. Heat vegetable oil in a large skillet or deep fryer to 350°F (180°C).
Dredge the eggplant slices in all-purpose flour, shaking off any excess.
Carefully add the eggplant slices to the hot oil and fry until golden brown and crispy, about 2-3 minutes per side. Fry the eggplant in batches if necessary. Once fried, transfer the eggplant slices to a plate lined with paper towels to drain excess oil.

In a separate saucepan, combine the dashi, soy sauce, mirin, sake, and sugar. Bring the mixture to a simmer over medium heat, then reduce the heat to low and let it simmer gently for about 5 minutes to allow the flavors to meld together. Place the fried eggplant slices in a serving dish or individual bowls. Pour the hot dashi broth over the eggplant slices.

Garnish the Nasu Agebitashi with thinly sliced green onions, toasted sesame seeds, and a sprinkle of shichimi togarashi for extra flavor and heat.

Serve the Nasu Agebitashi hot as a delicious appetizer or part of a traditional Japanese meal.

Enjoy the tender and crispy eggplant slices soaked in the flavorful dashi broth, perfect for a comforting and satisfying dish!

Inari Sushi (Sushi rice in tofu pouches)

Ingredients:

- 2 cups sushi rice
- 2 1/2 cups water
- 1/4 cup rice vinegar
- 2 tablespoons sugar
- 1 teaspoon salt
- 10-12 aburaage (fried tofu pouches)
- Toasted sesame seeds for garnish
- Thinly sliced green onions for garnish
- Optional fillings: cooked and seasoned vegetables, cooked shrimp, cooked egg strips, etc.

Instructions:

Rinse the sushi rice under cold water until the water runs clear. Drain well.

In a rice cooker or pot, combine the rinsed sushi rice and water. Cook the rice according to the manufacturer's instructions or until it's cooked and fluffy.

In a small saucepan, combine the rice vinegar, sugar, and salt. Heat over low heat, stirring occasionally, until the sugar and salt are dissolved. Remove from heat and let it cool.

Once the rice is cooked, transfer it to a large bowl. Gradually add the seasoned rice vinegar to the rice, folding gently to combine. Be careful not to smash the rice grains.

Let the seasoned sushi rice cool to room temperature while you prepare the aburaage tofu pouches.

Open each aburaage tofu pouch carefully to create a pocket without tearing the tofu.

Gently rinse the aburaage under cold water to remove excess oil and to soften them.

Pat the aburaage dry with paper towels, then gently squeeze out any excess water.

Stuff each aburaage pouch with a generous amount of seasoned sushi rice, gently pressing it down to fill the pouches completely.

Optional: Add your desired fillings such as cooked and seasoned vegetables, cooked shrimp, or cooked egg strips to the rice-filled pouches.

Sprinkle toasted sesame seeds and thinly sliced green onions on top of each filled pouch for garnish.

Serve the Inari Sushi at room temperature or chilled. Enjoy these delightful sushi treats as a snack, appetizer, or part of a Japanese-style meal.

Enjoy the sweet and savory flavors of Inari Sushi, perfect for sushi lovers looking for a unique and delicious variation!

Vegan Sukiyaki (Japanese hot pot)

Ingredients:

For the broth:

- 4 cups vegetable broth
- 1/4 cup soy sauce
- 1/4 cup mirin (Japanese sweet rice wine)
- 2 tablespoons sugar
- 2 cloves garlic, minced
- 1 teaspoon grated ginger

For the hot pot:

- 8 oz firm tofu, sliced
- 1/2 cup sliced shiitake mushrooms
- 1 cup sliced carrots
- 1 cup sliced napa cabbage
- 1 cup sliced green onions
- 1 cup sliced firm tofu or seitan
- 1 cup sliced konjac noodles or shirataki noodles (optional)
- 1 bunch enoki mushrooms, roots trimmed
- 1/2 cup sliced bamboo shoots (canned or fresh)
- 1 cup sliced bell peppers (any color)
- 1 cup sliced firm tofu or seitan
- 1 tablespoon vegetable oil for cooking

For serving:

- Cooked rice or noodles
- Soy sauce or ponzu sauce for dipping (optional)

Instructions:

In a large pot or hot pot, combine the vegetable broth, soy sauce, mirin, sugar, minced garlic, and grated ginger. Bring the mixture to a gentle boil over medium heat, then reduce the heat to low and let it simmer while you prepare the vegetables and tofu.

Arrange the sliced tofu, mushrooms, carrots, napa cabbage, green onions, konjac noodles (if using), enoki mushrooms, bamboo shoots, bell peppers, and additional tofu or seitan on a large platter or plate.

Heat a tablespoon of vegetable oil in a skillet or hot pot over medium heat. Add the sliced tofu or seitan to the skillet and cook until lightly browned on both sides, about 2-3 minutes per side. Remove from the skillet and set aside.

Arrange the prepared vegetables and tofu around the edge of the simmering broth in the hot pot. Let them cook for a few minutes until tender.

Once the vegetables are cooked to your liking, use chopsticks or a ladle to serve the hot pot ingredients into individual bowls. Serve with cooked rice or noodles on the side.

Enjoy the Vegan Sukiyaki hot pot with soy sauce or ponzu sauce for dipping, if desired.

Enjoy this comforting and flavorful Vegan Sukiyaki, perfect for a cozy meal with family and friends! Adjust the ingredients and seasonings to suit your taste preferences.

Vegan Oyakodon (Rice bowl with tofu and vegetables)

Ingredients:

For the broth:

- 1 cup vegetable broth
- 2 tablespoons soy sauce
- 1 tablespoon mirin (Japanese sweet rice wine)
- 1 tablespoon sugar
- 1/2 teaspoon grated ginger
- 1/2 teaspoon sesame oil

For the tofu and vegetables:

- 8 oz firm tofu, diced
- 1 onion, thinly sliced
- 1 cup sliced mushrooms (shiitake or button mushrooms)
- 1 cup sliced bell peppers (any color)
- 1 cup sliced green onions
- 1 tablespoon vegetable oil for cooking

For serving:

- Cooked Japanese rice
- Thinly sliced nori seaweed for garnish
- Thinly sliced green onions for garnish

Instructions:

In a small bowl, whisk together the vegetable broth, soy sauce, mirin, sugar, grated ginger, and sesame oil to make the broth. Set aside.

Heat vegetable oil in a large skillet or frying pan over medium heat. Add the diced tofu and cook until lightly browned on all sides, about 5-7 minutes. Remove the tofu from the skillet and set aside.

In the same skillet, add a bit more oil if needed, then add the thinly sliced onion. Cook until the onion is softened and translucent, about 3-4 minutes.

Add the sliced mushrooms and bell peppers to the skillet. Cook for another 3-4 minutes until the vegetables are tender.

Return the cooked tofu to the skillet, along with the sliced green onions.

Pour the prepared broth over the tofu and vegetables in the skillet. Bring the mixture to a simmer and let it cook for another 3-4 minutes, allowing the flavors to meld together.

Once the tofu and vegetables are heated through and the broth has slightly thickened, remove the skillet from the heat.

To serve, spoon the tofu and vegetable mixture over bowls of cooked Japanese rice.

Garnish the Vegan Oyakodon with thinly sliced nori seaweed and green onions.
Serve the Vegan Oyakodon hot and enjoy!

Enjoy this comforting and flavorful Vegan Oyakodon, a satisfying rice bowl dish perfect for a cozy meal! Adjust the ingredients and seasonings to suit your taste preferences.

Tofu Katsu Curry (Breaded tofu with Japanese curry)

Ingredients:

For the breaded tofu:

- 1 block firm tofu, drained and pressed
- Salt and pepper to taste
- All-purpose flour for dredging
- Vegan egg substitute (such as flaxseed meal or chickpea flour mixed with water)
- Panko breadcrumbs for coating
- Vegetable oil for frying

For the Japanese curry:

- 1 onion, chopped
- 2 carrots, diced
- 2 potatoes, diced
- 2 cups vegetable broth
- 2 tablespoons curry powder
- 1 tablespoon soy sauce
- 1 tablespoon mirin (Japanese sweet rice wine)
- 1 tablespoon sugar
- Salt to taste

Instructions:

Prepare the breaded tofu: Slice the pressed tofu into thick slices. Season with salt and pepper.

Set up a breading station with three shallow bowls: one containing all-purpose flour, one containing the vegan egg substitute, and one containing panko breadcrumbs.

Dredge each tofu slice in the flour, shaking off any excess. Dip them into the vegan egg substitute, then coat them evenly with the panko breadcrumbs, pressing gently to adhere.

Heat vegetable oil in a large skillet over medium-high heat. Once the oil is hot, carefully add the breaded tofu slices to the skillet. Fry until golden brown and crispy, about 3-4 minutes per side. Remove from the skillet and drain on paper towels.

Prepare the Japanese curry: In a large pot, heat a bit of vegetable oil over medium heat. Add the chopped onion and cook until softened, about 5 minutes. Add the diced carrots and potatoes to the pot, and sauté for another 5 minutes. Pour in the vegetable broth and bring to a simmer. Cook until the vegetables are tender, about 15-20 minutes.

Stir in the curry powder, soy sauce, mirin, sugar, and salt. Simmer for another 5 minutes to allow the flavors to meld together.

Once the curry is ready, remove it from heat.

Serve the breaded tofu slices alongside the Japanese curry. Optionally, you can serve them over cooked Japanese rice.

Enjoy your delicious Tofu Katsu Curry!

This recipe offers a vegan twist on the classic Japanese comfort food, providing a satisfying and flavorful meal. Adjust the ingredients and seasonings to suit your taste preferences.

Sunomono (Cucumber salad)

Ingredients:

- 2 cucumbers, thinly sliced
- 1/4 cup rice vinegar
- 2 tablespoons sugar
- 1 teaspoon soy sauce
- 1/2 teaspoon salt
- Toasted sesame seeds for garnish (optional)

Instructions:

In a small bowl, mix together the rice vinegar, sugar, soy sauce, and salt until the sugar and salt are dissolved.
Place the thinly sliced cucumbers in a large bowl.
Pour the vinegar mixture over the cucumbers and toss to coat evenly.
Cover the bowl and refrigerate the cucumber salad for at least 30 minutes to allow the flavors to meld together.
Before serving, garnish the Sunomono with toasted sesame seeds if desired.
Serve the Sunomono chilled as a refreshing side dish or appetizer.

Enjoy the crisp and tangy flavors of this classic Japanese cucumber salad, perfect for summer gatherings or alongside your favorite Japanese dishes!

Tofu Salad with Sesame Dressing

Ingredients:

For the salad:

- 1 block firm tofu, drained and pressed
- Mixed salad greens (such as lettuce, spinach, arugula)
- 1 cucumber, thinly sliced
- 1 carrot, julienned
- 1/4 cup sliced radishes
- 1/4 cup shredded red cabbage
- 2 green onions, thinly sliced
- Sesame seeds for garnish (optional)

For the sesame dressing:

- 3 tablespoons soy sauce
- 2 tablespoons rice vinegar
- 1 tablespoon sesame oil
- 1 tablespoon maple syrup or honey
- 1 teaspoon grated ginger
- 1 clove garlic, minced
- 1 tablespoon toasted sesame seeds

Instructions:

Prepare the tofu: Cut the pressed tofu into bite-sized cubes.
Heat a skillet over medium heat and lightly oil it. Add the tofu cubes and cook until golden brown on all sides, about 5-7 minutes. Remove from heat and set aside.
In a large salad bowl, combine the mixed salad greens, sliced cucumber, julienned carrot, sliced radishes, shredded red cabbage, and sliced green onions.
In a small bowl, whisk together the soy sauce, rice vinegar, sesame oil, maple syrup or honey, grated ginger, minced garlic, and toasted sesame seeds to make the sesame dressing.
Pour the sesame dressing over the salad and toss until everything is well coated.
Add the cooked tofu cubes to the salad and gently toss to combine.
Garnish the tofu salad with additional sesame seeds if desired.

Serve the tofu salad immediately as a delicious and nutritious meal.

Enjoy this Tofu Salad with Sesame Dressing, packed with flavor and nutrients, perfect for a light lunch or dinner option! Feel free to customize the salad with your favorite vegetables or add cooked grains for extra texture and heartiness.

Kombu Dashi (Seaweed broth)

Ingredients:

- 1 piece of kombu (dried kelp), about 4-6 inches in length
- 4 cups water

Instructions:

Start by wiping the surface of the kombu with a damp cloth to clean it. Avoid washing it under running water as it may remove some of the flavor.

Place the kombu in a pot with 4 cups of water. Allow it to soak for at least 30 minutes or up to several hours. This soaking process helps to extract the flavors and nutrients from the kombu.

After soaking, place the pot over medium heat. Slowly bring the water to a gentle simmer. Be careful not to let it boil vigorously, as this can cause the kombu to release a bitter flavor.

Just before the water reaches a boil, remove the kombu from the pot using a pair of tongs or a slotted spoon. Discard the kombu or reserve it for other uses, such as adding it to cooked dishes for extra flavor.

Allow the broth to simmer gently for an additional 5-10 minutes to further infuse the flavors.

After simmering, remove the pot from the heat and let the broth cool slightly.

Once cooled, strain the broth through a fine mesh sieve or cheesecloth to remove any remaining solids.

Your Kombu Dashi is now ready to use as a flavorful base for various Japanese dishes.

You can store leftover Kombu Dashi in the refrigerator for up to 3-4 days, or freeze it in ice cube trays for longer storage. Enjoy using this versatile and delicious broth in your cooking!

Vegan Tamago (Japanese egg substitute)

Ingredients:

- 1 block firm tofu
- 2 tablespoons nutritional yeast
- 1 tablespoon soy sauce
- 1 tablespoon mirin (Japanese sweet rice wine)
- 1 teaspoon sugar
- 1/2 teaspoon turmeric (for color)
- Vegetable oil for cooking

Instructions:

Start by draining the tofu and pressing it to remove excess moisture. You can do this by wrapping the tofu block in a clean kitchen towel and placing a heavy object on top for about 15-20 minutes.

In a bowl, crumble the pressed tofu into small pieces.

In a separate bowl, mix together the nutritional yeast, soy sauce, mirin, sugar, and turmeric to create the seasoning mixture.

Heat a bit of vegetable oil in a non-stick skillet over medium heat.

Add the crumbled tofu to the skillet and spread it out evenly.

Pour the seasoning mixture over the tofu in the skillet and stir to combine, ensuring that the tofu is evenly coated with the seasoning.

Cook the tofu mixture, stirring occasionally, until it is heated through and slightly browned, about 5-7 minutes.

Once the tofu mixture is cooked, transfer it to a rectangular mold (such as a sushi mold or small baking dish) lined with plastic wrap. Press the tofu mixture down firmly into the mold to shape it.

Allow the tofu mixture to cool in the mold for at least 30 minutes to set.

Once cooled and set, carefully remove the tofu block from the mold and slice it into thin rectangles to resemble Tamago.

Serve the vegan Tamago slices as a topping for sushi rolls, rice bowls, or enjoy them on their own as a flavorful snack or side dish.

This vegan Tamago alternative offers a similar texture and taste to the traditional Japanese omelette, making it a great option for those following a plant-based diet. Feel free to adjust the seasoning to suit your taste preferences!

Vegan Kakiage (Mixed vegetable tempura)

Ingredients:

- 1 small onion, thinly sliced
- 1 carrot, julienned
- 1 small sweet potato, peeled and thinly sliced
- 1 small zucchini, thinly sliced
- 1 cup thinly sliced mushrooms (such as shiitake or button mushrooms)
- 1 cup all-purpose flour
- 1 tablespoon cornstarch
- 1 teaspoon baking powder
- 1/2 teaspoon salt
- 3/4 cup ice-cold water
- Vegetable oil for frying
- Soy sauce or tempura dipping sauce for serving

Instructions:

In a large bowl, combine the sliced onion, carrot, sweet potato, zucchini, and mushrooms.
In a separate bowl, sift together the all-purpose flour, cornstarch, baking powder, and salt.
Gradually add the ice-cold water to the dry ingredients, whisking until you get a smooth batter. The batter should be thick but still pourable.
Add the mixed vegetables to the batter and gently mix until they are evenly coated.
Heat vegetable oil in a deep fryer or large pot to 350°F (180°C).
Using a large spoon or scoop, carefully drop spoonfuls of the vegetable mixture into the hot oil, making sure not to overcrowd the fryer. You may need to fry the vegetables in batches.
Fry the vegetable fritters until they are golden brown and crispy, about 2-3 minutes per side. Use a slotted spoon or wire mesh strainer to remove the fritters from the oil and transfer them to a plate lined with paper towels to drain excess oil.
Continue frying the remaining batches of vegetable fritters until all the batter is used up.
Serve the Vegan Kakiage hot, with soy sauce or tempura dipping sauce on the side for dipping.

Enjoy these crispy and flavorful Vegan Kakiage as a delightful appetizer or side dish! You can also serve them over a bed of steamed rice for a satisfying meal. Adjust the vegetables according to your preferences and availability.

Vegan Miso Ramen

Ingredients:

- 4 cups vegetable broth
- 2 cups water
- 3 tablespoons miso paste (white or yellow miso works well)
- 2 tablespoons soy sauce or tamari
- 2 cloves garlic, minced
- 1 tablespoon grated ginger
- 1 teaspoon sesame oil
- 8 ounces ramen noodles (check package to ensure they're vegan)
- Toppings of your choice (such as sliced green onions, tofu, mushrooms, spinach, corn, nori seaweed, bean sprouts, etc.)

Instructions:

In a large pot, bring the vegetable broth and water to a simmer over medium heat. In a small bowl, whisk together the miso paste, soy sauce, garlic, ginger, and sesame oil until smooth.

Add the miso mixture to the pot of simmering broth and stir well to combine. Let it simmer for about 5 minutes to allow the flavors to meld.

While the broth is simmering, cook the ramen noodles according to the package instructions. Drain and set aside.

Once the broth is ready, taste and adjust seasoning if needed.

To serve, divide the cooked noodles among serving bowls. Ladle the hot miso broth over the noodles.

Add your desired toppings on top of the ramen bowls.

Serve hot and enjoy your delicious vegan miso ramen!

Feel free to customize this recipe with your favorite vegetables and toppings to suit your taste preferences. Enjoy!

Vegan Okonomiyaki (Japanese savory pancake)

Ingredients:

- 2 cups shredded cabbage
- 1 cup grated carrot
- 3 spring onions, thinly sliced
- 1 cup all-purpose flour
- 1 teaspoon baking powder
- 1/2 teaspoon salt
- 1/4 teaspoon black pepper
- 3/4 cup water
- 2 tablespoons soy sauce or tamari
- 2 tablespoons vegan mayonnaise
- 2 tablespoons vegan Worcestershire sauce
- 1 tablespoon ketchup
- Optional toppings: chopped nori seaweed, pickled ginger, sesame seeds, extra vegan mayonnaise

Instructions:

In a large mixing bowl, combine the shredded cabbage, grated carrot, and sliced spring onions.
In a separate bowl, whisk together the all-purpose flour, baking powder, salt, pepper, water, and soy sauce until smooth.
Pour the flour mixture over the cabbage mixture and stir until well combined. The mixture should be thick and sticky.
Heat a non-stick skillet or griddle over medium heat and lightly oil the surface.
Spoon the cabbage mixture onto the skillet, forming pancakes about 4-5 inches in diameter. Flatten them gently with a spatula.
Cook the pancakes for about 4-5 minutes on each side, or until golden brown and crispy.
While the pancakes are cooking, prepare the sauce by combining the vegan mayonnaise, vegan Worcestershire sauce, and ketchup in a small bowl.
Once the pancakes are cooked, transfer them to a serving plate. Drizzle the sauce over the pancakes and sprinkle with optional toppings like chopped nori seaweed, pickled ginger, sesame seeds, and extra vegan mayonnaise.
Serve the vegan okonomiyaki immediately, and enjoy!

Feel free to customize your okonomiyaki with additional vegetables, tofu, or any other ingredients you like. It's a versatile dish that you can adapt to your taste preferences.

Tofu Poke Bowl

Ingredients:

For the Tofu:

- 1 block (14-16 ounces) extra-firm tofu, pressed and cubed
- 2 tablespoons soy sauce or tamari
- 1 tablespoon sesame oil
- 1 tablespoon rice vinegar
- 1 teaspoon grated ginger
- 1 clove garlic, minced

For the Poke Bowl:

- 2 cups cooked sushi rice or brown rice
- 1 avocado, sliced
- 1 cucumber, thinly sliced
- 1 cup shredded carrots
- 1 cup edamame, cooked
- 1 cup sliced radishes
- 1 cup shredded red cabbage
- 2 green onions, thinly sliced
- Sesame seeds, for garnish
- Nori seaweed, sliced thinly (optional)

For the Sauce:

- 2 tablespoons soy sauce or tamari
- 1 tablespoon sesame oil
- 1 tablespoon rice vinegar
- 1 teaspoon grated ginger
- 1 teaspoon honey or agave syrup (substitute with maple syrup for vegan option)
- 1 teaspoon sriracha or chili garlic sauce (adjust to taste)

Instructions:

Start by marinating the tofu. In a shallow dish, whisk together soy sauce, sesame oil, rice vinegar, grated ginger, and minced garlic. Add cubed tofu and gently toss to coat. Let it marinate for at least 15-30 minutes.

While the tofu is marinating, prepare the sauce by whisking together soy sauce, sesame oil, rice vinegar, grated ginger, honey or agave syrup, and sriracha or chili garlic sauce in a small bowl. Set aside.

Cook the sushi rice or brown rice according to package instructions. Once cooked, divide the rice evenly into serving bowls.

Arrange the marinated tofu, sliced avocado, cucumber, shredded carrots, edamame, sliced radishes, shredded red cabbage, and green onions on top of the rice in each bowl.

Drizzle the sauce over the tofu poke bowls.

Garnish with sesame seeds and thinly sliced nori seaweed, if desired.

Serve immediately and enjoy your delicious tofu poke bowl!

Feel free to customize your poke bowl with any additional toppings or vegetables you prefer. It's a versatile dish that you can make your own!

Vegan Yudofu (Hot tofu in broth)

Ingredients:

For the broth:

- 4 cups vegetable broth
- 2 cups water
- 4 dried shiitake mushrooms
- 1 piece of kombu (dried kelp), about 4 inches long
- 2 tablespoons soy sauce or tamari
- 1 tablespoon mirin (Japanese sweet rice wine)
- 1 teaspoon grated ginger

For the tofu:

- 1 block (14-16 ounces) firm tofu, drained and cut into cubes
- 2 green onions, thinly sliced (for garnish)
- Optional: grated daikon radish and soy sauce for dipping

Instructions:

In a large pot, combine the vegetable broth, water, dried shiitake mushrooms, kombu, soy sauce or tamari, mirin, and grated ginger. Bring to a simmer over medium heat.

Once the broth is simmering, reduce the heat to low and let it simmer gently for about 15-20 minutes to allow the flavors to meld. Stir occasionally.

While the broth is simmering, prepare the tofu. Cut the tofu into cubes and set aside.

After the broth has simmered for about 15-20 minutes, remove the kombu and dried shiitake mushrooms from the pot and discard them.

Gently add the tofu cubes to the broth and let them simmer for another 5 minutes, or until heated through.

Once the tofu is heated through, ladle the hot tofu and broth into individual serving bowls.

Garnish each bowl with thinly sliced green onions.

Serve the Vegan Yudofu hot as a comforting and nourishing meal. Optionally, you can serve grated daikon radish and soy sauce on the side for dipping the tofu.

Enjoy your Vegan Yudofu! It's a simple yet flavorful dish that's perfect for a cozy meal.

Vegan Chawanmushi (Savory egg custard)

Ingredients:

For the custard:

- 1 block (14-16 ounces) silken tofu
- 1 cup vegetable broth
- 1 tablespoon soy sauce or tamari
- 1 teaspoon mirin (Japanese sweet rice wine)
- 1/2 teaspoon salt
- 1/4 teaspoon sugar
- 1/2 teaspoon sesame oil
- 1/2 teaspoon grated ginger
- 1/2 teaspoon cornstarch (optional, for a firmer custard)
- 2 green onions, thinly sliced (for garnish)

Optional additions:

- Mushrooms, such as shiitake or enoki, thinly sliced
- Snow peas, blanched
- Carrots, thinly sliced and blanched
- Bamboo shoots, thinly sliced
- Other vegetables of your choice

Instructions:

Preheat your steamer. If you don't have a steamer, you can improvise by using a large pot with a lid and a steaming rack or a colander placed inside.
In a blender or food processor, combine the silken tofu, vegetable broth, soy sauce or tamari, mirin, salt, sugar, sesame oil, and grated ginger. Blend until smooth.
If you want a firmer custard, mix the cornstarch with a tablespoon of water to create a slurry. Stir the slurry into the tofu mixture until well combined.
Divide any optional additions evenly among the serving cups or ramekins.
Pour the tofu mixture into the serving cups or ramekins, filling them about 3/4 full.

Cover the cups or ramekins with aluminum foil or lids if available.

Place the cups or ramekins into the steamer or pot, ensuring there's enough space between them for the steam to circulate.

Steam the custards for about 15-20 minutes, or until they are set and no longer jiggly.

Once cooked, remove the custards from the steamer and let them cool slightly.

Garnish each custard with thinly sliced green onions before serving.

Serve the Vegan Chawanmushi warm as an appetizer or side dish.

Enjoy your Vegan Chawanmushi! It's a delicate and comforting dish perfect for any occasion.

Vegan Karaage (Japanese fried mock meat)

Ingredients:

For the marinade:

- 1 block (14-16 ounces) firm or extra-firm tofu, pressed and cut into bite-sized pieces
- 1/4 cup soy sauce or tamari
- 2 tablespoons rice vinegar
- 2 tablespoons sake (or mirin)
- 1 tablespoon grated ginger
- 2 cloves garlic, minced
- 1 teaspoon sesame oil
- 1 tablespoon maple syrup or agave syrup
- 1/4 teaspoon black pepper

For the coating:

- 1 cup all-purpose flour
- 1/2 cup cornstarch
- 1 teaspoon baking powder
- 1/2 teaspoon salt
- 1/4 teaspoon black pepper
- 1/2 cup cold water

For frying:

- Vegetable oil, for frying

Instructions:

In a mixing bowl, combine soy sauce or tamari, rice vinegar, sake or mirin, grated ginger, minced garlic, sesame oil, maple syrup or agave syrup, and black pepper. Whisk until well combined.

Add the tofu pieces to the marinade, making sure they are evenly coated. Cover the bowl and let it marinate in the refrigerator for at least 30 minutes, or up to 2 hours for more flavor.

In a separate bowl, prepare the coating by combining all-purpose flour, cornstarch, baking powder, salt, and black pepper. Mix well.

Gradually add cold water to the flour mixture, whisking continuously until you have a smooth batter. The batter should be thick enough to coat the tofu pieces, but still pourable.

Heat vegetable oil in a deep fryer or large pot to 350°F (180°C).

Remove the marinated tofu from the refrigerator. Dip each tofu piece into the batter, making sure it's evenly coated, then carefully drop it into the hot oil.

Fry the coated tofu pieces in batches, making sure not to overcrowd the fryer or pot. Fry for about 4-5 minutes, or until they are golden brown and crispy.

Use a slotted spoon or tongs to transfer the fried tofu pieces to a plate lined with paper towels to drain excess oil.

Repeat the frying process with the remaining tofu pieces until all are cooked.

Serve the Vegan Karaage hot, with your favorite dipping sauce or as part of a Japanese-inspired meal.

Enjoy your Vegan Karaage! It's crispy, flavorful, and perfect for serving as an appetizer or main dish.

Vegan Nigiri Sushi

Ingredients:

For the sushi rice:

- 1 cup sushi rice
- 1 1/4 cups water
- 2 tablespoons rice vinegar
- 1 tablespoon sugar
- 1/2 teaspoon salt

For the toppings (choose your favorites):

- Thinly sliced avocado
- Thinly sliced cucumber
- Thinly sliced carrot, lightly blanched
- Thinly sliced bell pepper
- Marinated tofu slices
- Vegan "smoked salmon" made from carrots or tomatoes
- Pickled vegetables (such as radish or ginger)

For assembling:

- Nori (seaweed) strips, optional
- Wasabi paste, optional
- Soy sauce or tamari, for dipping

Instructions:

Rinse the sushi rice under cold water until the water runs clear. Combine the rinsed rice and water in a rice cooker or pot and cook according to the manufacturer's instructions.
While the rice is cooking, prepare the sushi vinegar by combining rice vinegar, sugar, and salt in a small saucepan. Heat over low heat until the sugar and salt are dissolved. Remove from heat and let it cool.

Once the rice is cooked, transfer it to a large bowl and gently fold in the sushi vinegar mixture using a spatula or rice paddle. Be careful not to smash the rice grains. Allow the rice to cool to room temperature.

While the rice is cooling, prepare the toppings. Slice your chosen vegetables or tofu into thin pieces that will fit nicely on top of the rice.

Once the rice has cooled, dampen your hands with water and shape a small amount of rice into an oval-shaped ball. Press the rice firmly to hold its shape.

Place a small amount of wasabi paste (if using) on top of the rice ball, then place your chosen topping on top. If using nori strips, you can wrap them around the sides of the rice ball to secure the topping.

Repeat the process with the remaining rice and toppings until you have made desired number of nigiri sushi.

Serve the Vegan Nigiri Sushi with soy sauce or tamari for dipping.

Enjoy your Vegan Nigiri Sushi! It's a delicious and customizable dish that's perfect for sushi lovers.

Vegan Dorayaki (Sweet pancake with red bean paste)

Ingredients:

For the pancakes:

- 1 cup all-purpose flour
- 1 teaspoon baking powder
- 1/4 cup granulated sugar
- 3/4 cup plant-based milk (such as almond, soy, or oat milk)
- 1 tablespoon maple syrup or agave syrup
- 1 tablespoon vegetable oil
- 1/2 teaspoon vanilla extract

For the red bean paste filling:

- 1 cup cooked red beans (azuki beans)
- 1/4 cup granulated sugar
- 1 tablespoon vegetable oil

Instructions:

Start by making the red bean paste filling. In a saucepan, combine the cooked red beans and sugar. Cook over medium heat, stirring frequently, until the mixture thickens and becomes a paste-like consistency, about 10-15 minutes. Remove from heat and let it cool slightly.

In a mixing bowl, sift together the all-purpose flour and baking powder. Add the granulated sugar and mix well.

In a separate bowl, whisk together the plant-based milk, maple syrup or agave syrup, vegetable oil, and vanilla extract.

Pour the wet ingredients into the dry ingredients and mix until just combined. Be careful not to overmix; it's okay if there are a few lumps in the batter.

Heat a non-stick skillet or griddle over medium heat and lightly grease with vegetable oil or cooking spray.

Spoon about 2 tablespoons of batter onto the skillet to form a small pancake. Cook until bubbles form on the surface of the pancake and the edges begin to set, about 2-3 minutes.

Flip the pancake and cook for an additional 1-2 minutes, or until golden brown on both sides. Repeat with the remaining batter.

Once all the pancakes are cooked, assemble the dorayaki. Take one pancake and spread a spoonful of red bean paste filling onto the center. Place another pancake on top to sandwich the filling.

Repeat with the remaining pancakes and filling.

Serve the Vegan Dorayaki warm or at room temperature.

Enjoy your Vegan Dorayaki! It's a delightful treat that's perfect for dessert or snacking.

Vegan Matcha Tiramisu

Ingredients:

For the matcha sponge cake:

- 1 cup all-purpose flour
- 1 tablespoon matcha powder
- 1 teaspoon baking powder
- 1/4 teaspoon salt
- 3/4 cup granulated sugar
- 1/2 cup unsweetened applesauce
- 1/4 cup vegetable oil
- 1 teaspoon vanilla extract
- 1/2 cup plant-based milk (such as almond, soy, or oat milk)
- 1 tablespoon apple cider vinegar

For the matcha mascarpone cream:

- 1 1/2 cups vegan cream cheese (such as Tofutti or Daiya)
- 1/2 cup powdered sugar
- 1/4 cup coconut cream (the thick cream from a can of full-fat coconut milk)
- 2 tablespoons matcha powder
- 1 teaspoon vanilla extract

For assembly:

- 1 cup brewed strong coffee or espresso, cooled
- 2 tablespoons rum or coffee liqueur (optional)
- Cocoa powder, for dusting
- Vegan chocolate shavings, for garnish (optional)

Instructions:

Preheat your oven to 350°F (175°C). Grease and line an 8-inch square baking pan with parchment paper.

In a large mixing bowl, sift together the all-purpose flour, matcha powder, baking powder, and salt.

In another bowl, whisk together the granulated sugar, unsweetened applesauce, vegetable oil, and vanilla extract until well combined.

In a small bowl or measuring cup, mix together the plant-based milk and apple cider vinegar. Let it sit for a few minutes to curdle slightly.

Pour the wet ingredients (applesauce mixture and plant-based milk mixture) into the dry ingredients (flour mixture) and stir until just combined.

Pour the batter into the prepared baking pan and spread it out evenly.

Bake in the preheated oven for 20-25 minutes, or until a toothpick inserted into the center comes out clean.

While the cake is baking, prepare the matcha mascarpone cream. In a mixing bowl, beat together the vegan cream cheese, powdered sugar, coconut cream, matcha powder, and vanilla extract until smooth and creamy. Refrigerate until ready to use.

Once the cake is baked, remove it from the oven and let it cool completely in the pan.

Once the cake has cooled, cut it into small squares or rectangles to fit your serving glasses or dish.

In a shallow dish, mix together the cooled brewed coffee or espresso with rum or coffee liqueur (if using).

To assemble the tiramisu, dip each cake square briefly into the coffee mixture, making sure not to soak it too much.

Place a layer of dipped cake squares at the bottom of your serving glasses or dish.

Spread a layer of the matcha mascarpone cream over the cake layer.

Repeat the layers, alternating between dipped cake squares and matcha mascarpone cream, until you reach the top of the glasses or dish. Finish with a layer of mascarpone cream on top.

Cover the tiramisu with plastic wrap and refrigerate for at least 4 hours, or overnight, to allow the flavors to meld and the dessert to set.

Before serving, dust the top with cocoa powder and garnish with vegan chocolate shavings, if desired.

Serve chilled and enjoy your Vegan Matcha Tiramisu!

This vegan twist on classic tiramisu is sure to impress with its unique matcha flavor and creamy texture.

Milton Keynes UK
Ingram Content Group UK Ltd.
UKHW051055220424
441551UK00015B/1023